21st Century

MYSTERIES OF DEEP SPACE

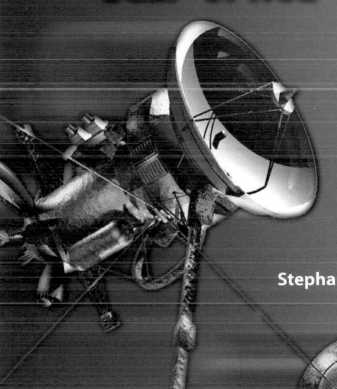

Stephanie Paris

Consultants

Timothy Rasinski, Ph.D.
Kent State University

Lori Oczkus
Literacy Consultant

Matt Heverly
NASA Engineer

Based on writing from
TIME For Kids. *TIME For Kids* and the *TIME For Kids* logo are registered trademarks of TIME Inc. Used under license.

Publishing Credits

Dona Herweck Rice, *Editor-in-Chief*
Lee Aucoin, *Creative Director*
Jamey Acosta, *Senior Editor*
Lexa Hoang, *Designer*
Stephanie Reid, *Photo Editor*
Rane Anderson, *Contributing Author*
Rachelle Cracchiolo, *M.S.Ed., Publisher*

Image Credits: cover, pp.3–5, 8–11, 16–21, 28–29, 32–33, 33, 36, 36–39, 44–45, 45, 48–49, 53 (left), 54–64 NASA; p.26 (bottom) iStockphoto; pp.23 (bottom), 55 REUTERS/Newscom; p.38 ZUMA Press/Newscom pp.23 (top), 36, 42, 46–48, 50–51, 64 (bottom) Photo Researchers Inc.; p.35 (illustration) Stephanie Reid; pp.30–31, 37, 40–41 (illustrations) Timothy J. Bradley; All other images from Shutterstock.

Teacher Created Materials

5301 Oceanus Drive
Huntington Beach, CA 92649-1030
http://www.tcmpub.com
ISBN 978-1-4333-4900-3

TABLE OF CONTENTS

WHAT'S OUT THERE?

When you look up at the night sky, what do you think about? Do you imagine visiting those faraway stars? Do you wonder if there is life out there? Do you wonder how many stars there are and where they all came from? These are the same questions that scientists ask.

In the 20th century, adventurers began to explore space. They built powerful rockets. They sent satellites to faraway places. In the 1960s, they even sent humans to the moon! But it's the 21st century now. Technology is more advanced. And scientists are setting goals that take us farther away from home.

THINK LINK

- Why do scientists want to explore space?
- How has learning about space changed our lives?
- What advances in technology have helped scientists explore space in the 21st century?

THE SUN

A star lies at the center of our **solar system**. It's only a midsized yellow star. Yet a million Earths could fit inside. Its **mass** is nearly 300,000 times greater than the Earth's. We call it the *sun*. Without the sun, Earth would be cold and very dark. The sun's hot bright energy allows life on Earth to survive. Without the sun's **gravity**, Earth and the other **planets** orbiting our sun would fly off into space. Without the sun, there would be nothing to see— and no one to see it.

SHINE YOUR LIGHT

The color of a star is related to how big it is. This is because the color is related to the temperature and the temperature is related to the size.

White Stars	Blue Stars	Yellow Stars	Red Dwarfs
75,000°F	45,000°F	10,000°F	less than 7,000°F
as small as Earth; same mass as the sun	much larger than the sun; burns brightly and quickly	the same size as the sun; stable and slow burning	nearly a tenth of the mass of the sun; the most common type of star

More than 99 percent of the solar system's mass is found in the sun.

WE ARE ALL STARDUST

Nearly every **element** in the universe was created in an intensely hot star. Older stars exploded and sent these element into the universe. In time, they mixed together to create new stars, new planets, and even life here on Earth.

A STAR IS BORN

Just like humans, stars have a life cycle. They are born, grow, and eventually die. But unlike humans, a star's life cycle can last millions of years. Just like humans, stars die at different ages. Humans die when their bodies wear out. Stars die when they run out of fuel.

A smaller sun-like star is formed.

As it grows older, the star expands into a **red giant**.

Stars begin as giant clouds of dust and gas. These **nebulae** are the birthplaces of stars.

Low-Mass Star Life Cycle

A planetary nebula is formed as the dying star casts off its outer layers of gas.

The star becomes a **white dwarf** as its core begins to cool and shrink.

When all its energy is used, the star becomes a **black dwarf**.

8

A massive star is formed.

As the star produces less energy, it forms a red giant.

Massive Star Life Cycle

Some explosions cause dust and gas to expand across large areas. A new nebula is formed.

When the star's core collapses, the star explodes in a **supernova**.

After an explosion, a dense **neutron star** may form.

The largest stars collapse into **black holes**. Here, gravity is so strong that nothing, not even light, can escape.

INNER PLANETS

Eight planets orbit the sun. Over a hundred moons have been discovered. There are nearly a million **asteroids** and billions of **comets**. How can we learn about all of these places and objects?

Mercury and Venus are the planets closest to the sun. Both have extreme temperatures. This makes landing spacecraft there challenging. But scientists have sent two **probes** to visit these inner planets. In the 1970s, the United States sent the Mariner 10 probe. It sent back photos and information. Technology has improved. Today, the Messenger probe is visiting the two planets directly.

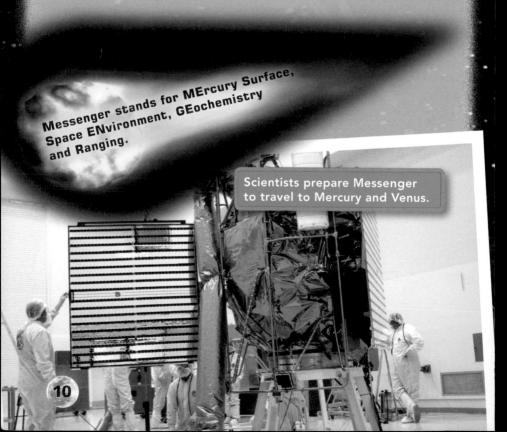

Messenger stands for MErcury Surface, Space ENvironment, GEochemistry and Ranging.

Scientists prepare Messenger to travel to Mercury and Venus.

The Cassini-Huygens spacecraft was launched in 1997. After seven years, it reached Saturn, and the Cassini orbiter released the Huygens probe to the surface of Titan, one of Saturn's moons. The probe is expected to continue transmitting **data** until 2017.

PROBING QUESTIONS

A probe is an unmanned spacecraft. It has special instruments that collect data. Then, it sends back what it has learned to scientists on Earth. Scientists who design the instruments sometimes have to wait for years to find out if everything they sent with the probe will work.

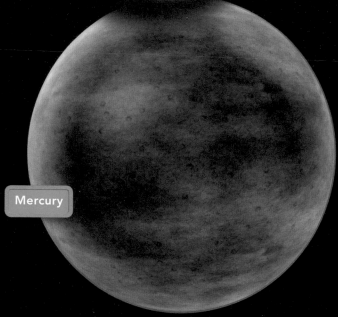

Eighteen Mercury-sized planets could fit inside one Earth.

Mercury

MERCURY

Mercury is the closest planet to the sun. It's a small rocky place that's hard to see from Earth. It is often hidden by the sun's glare. The surface of Mercury is covered with hard wrinkles. Scientists believe they were formed when the planet cooled millions of years ago. This planet has a very thin atmosphere. That causes it to have the wildest temperature changes of any planet in the solar system.

VENUS

Venus is sometimes called Earth's twin. It's not only the closest planet to Earth. It's also the most similar. Both planets are about the same size. They are made up of many of the same things. The most important difference is found in the air rather than on the ground. Venus's atmosphere is made of **sulfuric acid**. There is also **carbon dioxide**. These two chemicals are deadly for humans to breathe.

Venus

Venus rotates so slowly that more than a hundred Earth days pass before Venus starts another day.

ROUND AND ROUND

Venus spins clockwise. This is the opposite of the other planets in our solar system. That means that on Venus, the sun rises in the west and sets in the east!

Venus

other planets

MARS

Mars has intrigued people for many years. The ancients could easily find the red planet in the sky. Later, scientists noticed narrow lines on its surface. People imagined they were **canals** built by an alien race. Better images proved the "canals" were just an **optical illusion**. But the red planet still fascinates us today. Recently, scientists found **evidence** of water on Mars. They have also found hints that bacteria may have lived on the red planet. If this is true, it would be the first evidence of life anywhere other than Earth!

A SECOND HOME

Outside of Earth, Mars is the planet friendliest to human life. There is very little air, and it is very cold. But it has days that are just a little longer than 24 hours. The rocky, red ground is suitable to stand on. But its seasons are twice as long as Earth's. If there really is water, explorers from Earth may one day be able to use it to survive for years at a time.

CURIOUSER AND CURIOUSER

On August 6, 2012 the rover Curiosity landed on Mars. This robot is designed to act as an explorer, a chemist, a geologist, and a photographer. It is collecting data to help scientists learn if life may have once existed on Mars.

No one has visited Mars yet, but three rovers have landed on the planet and sent back information.

MAPPING THE SOLAR SYSTEM

In the future, humans may build homes on other planets. Scientists are slowly mapping the solar system. Every mission teaches us more about what's in the neighborhood.

Mars

Mars looks red because the soil has a lot of iron oxide in it. That's rust.

Venus

There are over 1,600 volcanoes on Venus.

Earth

Mercury

Mercury's temperatures vary more than any other planet's. During the day, they can reach highs of 427°C. At night, they dip to -183°C!

Neptune

Neptune has the largest orbit. It takes over 164 Earth years to go once around the sun!

Uranus

When Uranus was first discovered, scientists thought it was just another star.

Saturn

Many scientists think that one of Saturn's moons, Titan, might contain life below its icy exterior.

Jupiter

Jupiter has more than twice as much mass than all the other planets combined!

What lies beyond? Scientists can't wait to answer this question!

OUTER PLANETS

The four planets farthest from the sun are known as the *outer planets*. All four are giant planets made of gas. Compared to Earth, they're huge. They're impossible to miss, but they're very distant. Even when Neptune moves closer to Earth, it's still 2.7 billion miles away! And it took more than a year for the New Horizons spacecraft to reach Jupiter in 2007.

Jupiter

MASTER OF THE MOONIVERSE

With more than 60 moons, Jupiter appears to have more moons than any other planet in the solar system.

JUPITER

The largest planet in the solar system is home to one of the fiercest storms in the **galaxy**. Earth's surface is rocky. But Jupiter is mostly gas and liquid. Colorful stripes show where constant storms and large clouds spin through the sky. The giant red spot is just one of Jupiter's hurricanes. It's wider than the entire width of the Earth! This intense storm has been observed in **telescopes** for more than 300 years.

Because of the stronger gravity on Jupiter, if you weigh 90 pounds on Earth, you would weigh over 200 pounds on Jupiter.

SATURN

Saturn is also a gas giant. For hundreds of years, people have admired the beautiful rings of Saturn. Astronomers report the rings are made of bits of ice, rock, and dust. Over the years, they have found more than 60 moons in Saturn's orbit.

VOYAGERS

In 1977, the National Aeronautics and Space Administration (NASA) launched space probes Voyager 1 and Voyager 2. They were expected to go on a five-year mission to explore Jupiter and Saturn. But the Voyager probes were stronger than anyone imagined. They continue to explore new worlds still today. Voyager 2 is the only probe to have visited Uranus and Neptune. Both crafts are nearing the edges of our solar system. They appear to have enough power to send back data until 2020.

Saturn

Astronomers say the pull from Saturn's moons helps the particles in the rings remain around Saturn.

GOLDEN RECORDS

The Voyager probes are carrying golden **phonograph** records. These records are meant to show what life is like on Earth to any aliens that might find them. There are diagrams of the solar system and images of people and animals. There are samples of music and even whale songs.

URANUS

In 1781, Uranus was the first planet to be discovered with a telescope. It's one of the coldest planets in the solar system. The average temperature is -371.2°F. That's about three times colder than any temperature discovered on Earth! A day on Uranus is just 17 hours long. Uranus has 27 moons. It has beautiful rings, too. Saturn and Uranus have many things in common.

THE SIDEWAYS PLANET

Most planets spin vertically on their axes. But Uranus tilts on its side as it spins.

Uranus

other planets

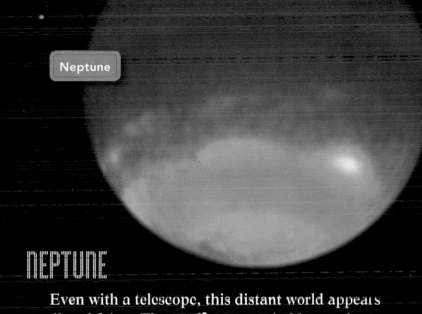

Neptune

NEPTUNE

Even with a telescope, this distant world appears small and faint. The **methane** gas in Neptune's atmosphere makes it look blue. Neptune is thought to have a rocky core. Icy water, **ammonia**, and methane surround the core. Voyager 2 traveled closer to the planet than ever before.

BLOWN AWAY

Neptune is a stormy world. Scientists have observed winds blowing up to 1,200 miles per hour. The strongest cyclone recorded on Earth happened in Australia in 1996. Winds there blew only 253 miles per hour.

THE FORGOTTEN PLANET

Pluto was first discovered in 1930. Astronomers called it the "ninth planet." At first, it seemed similar to other planets. But then, scientists found many icy objects out past Neptune. Scientists created a more precise definition of a planet, and Pluto didn't qualify. Unlike planets, Pluto orbits the sun in the midst of **debris**. Because of these things, Pluto is classified as a dwarf planet.

Neptune

WHAT IS A PLANET?

- Planets orbit stars like the sun.
- They have enough gravity to be spherical in shape.
- Planets "clear the neighborhood" around them. This means that they have enough gravity to remove nearby debris to create a clean orbit.

Pluto's radius is only about $\frac{1}{20}$ the size of Neptune's radius.

"What we know about Pluto could fit on the back of a postage stamp. The textbooks will be rewritten when this mission is complete. The true nature of the mission is to find the answer to questions we don't even know how to ask."

—Colleen Hartman, a NASA scientist discussing the 2006 launch of the New Horizons probe to Pluto

COMETS

When comets are deep in space, they're very stable. But when they near the sun, they become glowing balls of dust. Until recently, we knew very little about comets. In 1986, the European Space Agency (ESA) sent out the Giotto spacecraft to study Halley's Comet. It sent back more than 2,000 images. Six years later, it sent back information from another comet. In 2014, scientists plan to send another probe that can land on an active comet.

AEROGEL

This light-weight substance is the only thing able to collect comet particles without damaging them. Aerogel looks as if you could pass your hand right through it. But it feels like hard foam when you touch it.

aerogel

ASTEROIDS

Millions of rocky objects lie between Mars and Jupiter. Some are large. Others are very small. Sometimes, one of these objects leaves the asteroid belt and heads into space. It may strike a planet. If a large asteroid hits Earth, it could cause huge problems—like mass extinction!

ASTEROID ALERT!

An asteroid is hurtling toward Earth! A small band of brave heroes takes a rocket up and blows the asteroid into a thousand pieces—Earth is saved! That's how it happens in the movies. But in real life, blowing the asteroid to pieces would just mean more pieces would hit Earth. This could actually be worse. Scientists say a better plan might be to gently nudge the asteroid out of the way.

WATCHING AND LISTENING

Space is filled with enough objects to keep us learning for a hundred lifetimes. Or more! So how do we learn about these objects that are millions of miles from Earth? Some can be seen with the naked eye. That's how early astronomers studied the night sky. With their simple observations, their curiosity grew. Today, we use more advanced technology. Some is here on Earth. The rest is in outer space.

Crew members prepare for the first manned spaceflight not run by a government agency.

"Space is big. You just won't believe how vastly, hugely, mind-bogglingly big it is. I mean, you may think it's a long way down the road to the drugstore, but that's just peanuts next to space."

—Douglas Adams, writer

THE ELECTROMAGNETIC SPECTRUM

Electromagnetic radiation is energy that fills the universe. The electromagnetic spectrum is made up of different wavelengths. Each type of wavelength helps us "see" different parts of the universe. The electromagnetic spectrum is made up of seven types of wavelengths: radio waves, microwaves, infrared waves, visible light waves, ultraviolet waves, X-rays, and gamma waves. Read below to find out more about these different wavelengths and how they are used.

Microwaves are used to cook food. This is how microwave ovens got their name.

wavelength

radio waves	microwaves	infrared waves

10^2 1meter 10^{-1} 10^{-2} 10^{-3} 10^{-4}

Radio waves are used to send radio signals, TV signals, and even cell phone signals.

Infrared waves come in many forms. Some infrared waves produce the heat you feel from a fire.

STOP! THINK...

- Which wavelengths are visible to humans?

- Which wavelengths are shortest? Which waves are longest?

- Why do you think humans are only able to see some types of energy?

Some of the largest galaxies in the universe are strong sources of X-rays.

| visible light | ultraviolet waves | X-rays | gamma waves |

10^{-5} 10^{-6} 10^{-7} 10^{-8} 10^{-9} 10^{-10} 10^{-11} $1($

Hot objects such as the sun are powerful sources of ultraviolet radiation.

Gamma rays can be produced by supernovas.

TELESCOPES

Telescopes were some of the first tools used for viewing objects in space. They're still among the best. At first, telescopes were just tubes with a series of glass lenses inside them. But the glass was hard to grind perfectly. And it was heavy. Then, people learned they could use mirrors to solve these problems. Today, high-tech telescopes also use computers to analyze the images.

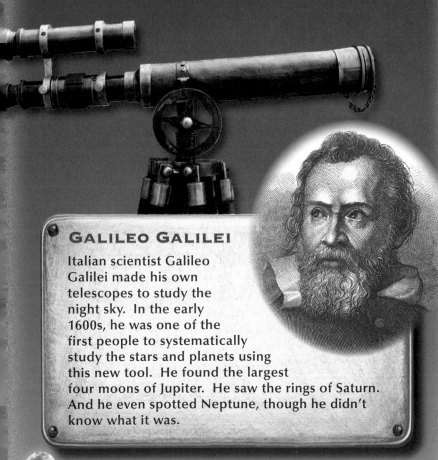

GALILEO GALILEI

Italian scientist Galileo Galilei made his own telescopes to study the night sky. In the early 1600s, he was one of the first people to systematically study the stars and planets using this new tool. He found the largest four moons of Jupiter. He saw the rings of Saturn. And he even spotted Neptune, though he didn't know what it was.

WHAT'S IN A NAME?

Today, calling a scientist by his last name is a sign of respect. So why do we call Galileo by his first name? Because that's what he called himself. This Italian scientist lived in Italy during a time where **surnames** were optional. Instead, he would say, "I am Galileo, son of Vincenzo." Or he might have said, "I am Galileo of Florence."

SPACE TELESCOPES

Earth's atmosphere can bend or bounce light that is coming toward us. This is good for life on Earth. It protects us from harmful radiation. But it is not so good for being able to see objects in space. So scientists have sent a few special telescopes into space itself. This lets them see distant light without interference from the atmosphere.

THE REFLECTING TELESCOPE

Telescope is a Greek word that means "seeing far." A few hundred years ago, the first telescopes were made with lenses. But scientists wanted to see distant objects more clearly. The reflecting telescope allowed astronomers to see other galaxies. They discovered the universe is expanding. Using reflecting telescopes changed our idea of the universe and Earth's place in it.

1 Light enters the open end of the reflecting telescope.

secondary mirror

3 The secondary mirror reflects and focuses the light into a slit in the primary mirror.

focal point

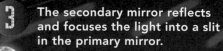

LIGHT-YEAR

A **light-year** is the distance that light can travel in one year. Light travels very fast. But it still takes time to get from one place to another. This means that when we are looking at the night sky, we are actually looking back in time! The farther away something is, the further back in time we are seeing it. If an object is 1,000 light-years away, then the light we see from it was made 1,000 years ago!

2 Light waves travel to a curved mirror.

primary mirror

eyepiece

4 The viewer sees a distant object through the eye piece.

THE HUBBLE SPACE TELESCOPE

On April 24, 1990, NASA launched a space telescope about the size of a school bus. Images from the Hubble Space Telescope can be startling in their detail and beauty. But they're not always exactly the way we would see them with our naked eye. From Earth, distant stars look like dots of light. But the Hubble Telescope can zoom in. It's like one giant eye in the sky.

EXPANDING UNIVERSE

The Hubble Space Telescope is named after astronomer Edwin P. Hubble. He is famous for discovering the universe is expanding. This led to the development of the **Big Bang Theory**. One of the Hubble Telescope's biggest discoveries is that the universe continues to expand—faster than it used to!

HUBBLE HOW TO

1 The telescope sensors record light from a distant object.

2 Black-and-white images are sent back to Earth. Scientists on the ground use computer programs to analyze the information and combine the photos.

4 The colors can be used to show what the object might really look like. Or they can be used to bring out details or highlight important information.

3 They usually have three images to combine and assign a different color to each one.

OTHER OBSERVATORIES

Not all information that reaches Earth from space is in the form of visible light. Objects in space send out many kinds of energy. Gas giants send out radio waves. The sun sends out sound waves. Some objects send out gamma rays and gravity waves. **Observatories** in space and on Earth are looking for all these and more.

THE SOUTH POLE TELESCOPE

The South Pole isn't just cold. During the winter, the sun never rises. The air there is extremely dry because all the moisture freezes. This makes it a perfect place to observe space. The South Pole Telescope monitors radiation from space. Scientists use the information to analyze any variations for clues about the Big Bang.

FERMI GAMMA-RAY SPACE TELESCOPE

The Fermi telescope was an international effort. It has a Large Area Telescope (LAT) and a Gamma-ray Burst Monitor. The data collected will help scientists answer questions about some of the most mysterious places in the universe.

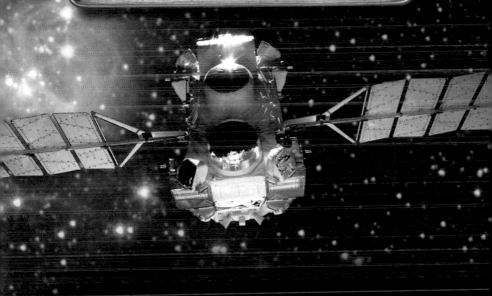

The Solar and Heliospheric Observatory (SOHO) project was designed to study the structure of the sun, its atmosphere, and solar wind. Large radio dishes around the world command the spacecraft and download data.

OUR PLACE IN SPACE

What lies beyond our solar system? How do events in the universe affect us on Earth? Does life exist on other planets? How can we learn more about these things when the universe is so big?

Powerful telescopes have been built. And many of our questions are beginning to be answered. Scientists can measure the distances to other galaxies. Now, all they need to do is build the spaceships to get us there!

NEXT-DOOR NEIGHBORS

The closest star to Earth is Proxima Centauri. Its name means "nearest to." It is about 4.2 light-years away and has a much lower mass than our sun. It is part of a triple-star-system. The star system is made up of three stars. All three stars orbit around each other.

> "Somewhere, something incredible is waiting to be known."
>
> —Carl Sagan, scientist

It takes Alpha Centuri A and B about 80 years to rotate around each other. Proxima Centauri takes about 500,000 years to rotate around those stars.

Proxima Centauri

Alpha Centauri A   **Alpha Centauri B**

CONSTELLATIONS

Stargazers have long noticed patterns in the sky. The stars seemed to move across the sky in groups. When people looked up at the night sky, they imagined wonderful stories. Some believed the stars were heroes honored by a place in the heavens.

Long ago, astronomers divided the sky into 12 parts. This helped them find groups of stars in the sky. In each section, they saw pictures in the stars. In different parts of the world, people saw different pictures. But the ones most familiar today are those used by the Romans.

THE SUN AND MOON

People created stories about the sun and the moon, too. One group believed the sun was a fiery chariot driven by a god. One tale said the moon was broken into pieces by an angry rival, later to be put back together by its lover.

STAR SIGNS

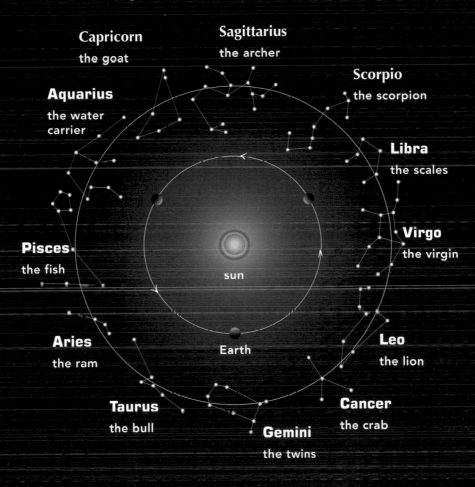

Capricorn
the goat

Sagittarius
the archer

Scorpio
the scorpion

Aquarius
the water
carrier

Libra
the scales

Pisces
the fish

Virgo
the virgin

sun

Aries
the ram

Earth

Leo
the lion

Taurus
the bull

Cancer
the crab

Gemini
the twins

A SIGN OF THE TIMES

Early peoples used constellations to
help with planting and harvesting. For
example, when the signs of Taurus,
Virgo, and Capricorn were in the
sky, they knew to plant crops such as
carrots and potatoes.

DIG DEEPER!

STARGAZING

This chart shows some of the major constellations and how to find them in the night sky during the winter. Face south and hold the chart up over your head. The directions look backwards here, but when held overhead, they'll line up right. Look for the stars as they appear on the chart. Note: This chart is for the Northern Hemisphere. If you are in the Southern Hemisphere, you will need a different chart.

East

VIRGO

CORVUS

Orion

Orion is one of the easiest constellations to find. It shows a hunter wearing a belt. One of the reasons it is easy to spot is because it has two very bright stars in it.

North

Polaris

Polaris is often called the North Star or the Pole Star. Because of its position in the sky, it seems to always be directly above Earth's North Pole. If you watch the night sky, it looks as if all the other stars rotate around it and Polaris never seems to move.

West

South

GALAXIES

A galaxy is a huge system of stars held together by gravity. There are at least 100 billion in our universe! They come in an amazing variety of shapes and sizes. Our own Milky Way galaxy is shaped like a spiral. Scientists think it was formed about 10 billion years ago. The Milky Way is surrounded by a group of about 50 other galaxies. Since they're the ones closest to us, they're called the Local Group.

Galaxies outside the Milky Way are too far away to visit. But we're getting a good idea what they may be like. Scientists use special equipment to see things our naked eye cannot.

Look into the sky without using a telescope. All the stars you see are stars within the Milky Way galaxy.

No one is really sure how many stars are in the Milky Way. Most think it's somewhere in the billions.

the Milky Way as imagined by an artist

THE LARGER PICTURE

Our solar system is huge. It holds 8 planets, more than 150 moons, the sun, and more. But it's only a tiny fraction of the Milky Way galaxy. If the solar system were the size of a marble, the rest of the Milky Way would be nearly half the size of Canada.

Galaxies are grouped by shape. Spiral galaxies are shaped like our Milky Way. They're flat disks with trailing arms. Elliptical galaxies are thought to be the oldest galaxies. They're round or oval and have red and yellow stars. Irregular galaxies do not have any obvious shape. They may be starting to form arms. But mostly they're just gas, dust, and hot blue stars.

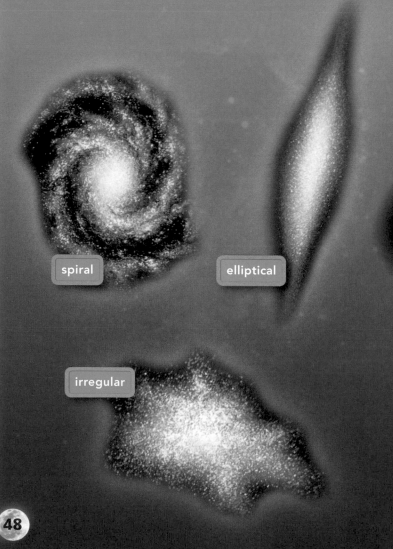

spiral

elliptical

irregular

WHEN GALAXIES COLLIDE

Sometimes, gravity pulls galaxies into each other, and the galaxies collide. Since these collisions happen over billions of years, what scientists see is just a snapshot of the action.

This image was taken by the Hubble Space Telescope in 2008. It is thought to show two galaxies combining after crashing together.

THE UNIVERSE

The universe is, simply put, *everything*. It's all the planets, stars, matter, and the space in between them. It's everything we know about—and all the things we haven't discovered yet. One of the goals of space explorers is to figure out the true nature of the universe. How did it begin? How will it end? How big is it really? These are tricky questions, but scientists are learning more every day.

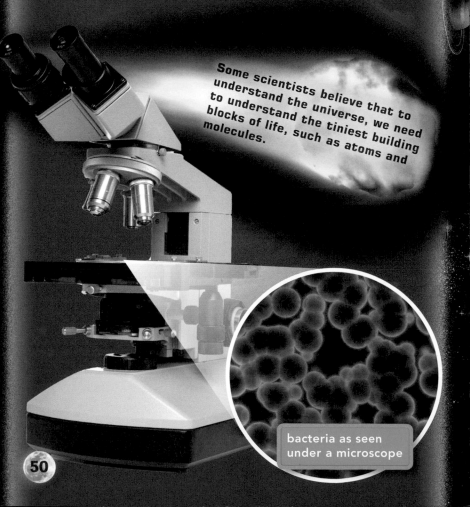

Some scientists believe that to understand the universe, we need to understand the tiniest building blocks of life, such as atoms and molecules.

bacteria as seen under a microscope

HOW MANY STARS?

If one galaxy has billions upon billions of stars, how many stars are in the universe? No one knows for sure. But the current best estimate is about 300 sextillion. That is 300,000,000,000,000,000,000,000 stars!

A BILLION BIRTHDAYS

Scientists believe the universe is about 13.7 billion years old.

THE SEARCH FOR LIFE

Is there life somewhere other than Earth? And if there is life "out there," what is the best way to look for it? One way is to look for planets similar to Earth. We know that life exists here. So maybe it will exist in places that are similar.

Exoplanets are planets that exist outside the solar system. Scientists look for planets that are in the habitable zone. That is the area around a star where life can thrive. In this area, it's not too hot or too cold. A planet with liquid water would be ideal.

EXTREME LIFE FORMS

Sometimes, exploring our own planet can give us better ideas about what might be elsewhere. In 2005, NASA scientists examined ice samples dating back 32,000 years. Not only did they find a new species of bacteria, but it was still alive! This discovery caused scientists to rethink their ideas about where life outside Earth might be found. Just because a place is frozen doesn't mean life can't exist there.

CALLING ALL ALIENS!

Do you want to help search for extraterrestrial intelligence? The Search for Extraterrestrial Intelligence (SETI) is a project that has brought people together from around the world. They all have a common goal: finding intelligent life in space. Want to help? Hop on your computer and join up with SETI to form a super-computer that's calling all aliens!

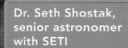

Dr. Seth Shostak, senior astronomer with SETI

53

WORKING TOGETHER

Scientists around the world are working together to learn more about space. Discoveries are happening faster than ever before. No one knows what we may find. That is what makes exploring space so exciting. What will the 22nd century bring? Will we find life on other planets? Will we settle a colony on Mars? The time to start exploring is now.

American astronaut
Joseph Acaba and
Russian cosmonauts
Gennady Padalka and
Sergei Revin join hands.

DIG DEEPER!

WE HAVE LIFTOFF

The 21st century has just begun, but we have already learned some amazing things about our solar system and beyond. Take a look at this time line. If you were to design a mission into space, what would you want it to explore?

1977
Voyager 1 and 2 are launched to study Jupiter, Saturn, and beyond.

2011
Scientists detect oceans of cold water vapor surrounding a new star. Scientists believe this star may someday have planets like Earth with liquid water.

2011
Scientists working with the Kepler Space Telescope find two Earth-size planets orbiting a distant star. They also find a larger planet in the habitable zone of another star.

2008

After much analysis, it is confirmed that frozen water exists on Mars.

2016?

The Square Kilometer Array begins searching for extraterrestrial life.

2005

Scientists analyze samples of ice that is 32,000 years old. They find living bacteria, leading to new questions about where to look for life.

2030s?

Humans visit Mars.

2012

The Curiosity rover lands on Mars.

2018?

Europe's Extremely Large Telescope is scheduled to begin operation.

GLOSSARY

ammonia—a colorless gas with a strong smell and taste

asteroids—rocks orbiting around the sun

Big Bang Theory—a scientific theory that the universe was created billions of years ago as a result of a giant explosion

black dwarf—the remains of a white dwarf after it cools and no longer emits visible light

black holes—invisible regions in space with strong gravitational fields

canals—waterways built for navigation or irrigation

carbon dioxide—a colorless gas that is formed especially by the burning and breaking down of live substances

comets—medium-size icy masses of gas, dust, and water orbiting the sun

constellations—groupings of stars that have been given names based on the way they look

data—information

debris—the remains of something broken down or destroyed

electromagnetic radiation—electrical or magnetic energy that fills the universe, ranging from gamma rays to radio waves and including visible light

element—one of the basic pieces that make up objects in the universe

evidence—an outward sign that tends to prove or disprove something

exoplanets—planets outside our solar system

galaxy—a system of stars, dust, and gas held together by gravity

gravity—the force of attraction between two objects that have mass

light-year—the distance that light travels in one year or about 6 trillion miles

mass—a measure of the amount of matter, or material, within an object

methane—a colorless, odorless, flammable gas that is produced by decaying matter

nebulae—huge clouds of gas or dust in deep space

neutron star—a very dense star that is produced by the collapse of a much larger star

observatories—buildings that hold large telescopes

optical illusion—an image that appears different from the way it is in reality

phonograph—an instrument that reproduces sounds recorded on a grooved disk

planets—bodies that orbit around a star after clearing the space around them

probes—spacecrafts designed to explore the solar system and send data back to Earth

red giant—the remains of a sun-like star once it begins to lose fuel and glow red

solar system—a set of planets or other bodies orbiting a star (such as the sun)

spectrum—a continuous range or series

sulfuric acid—a strong acid that is colorless and eats away at many solid substances

supernova—a huge explosion that can occur as a star begins to die

surnames—last names shared by family members

telescopes—tools for viewing distant objects

white dwarf—a final stage of a glowing star, when the leftover core begins to cool and shrink

INDEX

BIBLIOGRAPHY

Aguilar, David A. *Planets, Stars, and Galaxies: A Visual Encyclopedia of Our Universe.* **National Geographic Society, 2007.**

Discover the mysteries of deep space. Full-page color photographs, star charts, moon maps, and fun facts bring the outer reaches of the universe straight to your fingertips.

Carson, Mary Kay. *Exploring the Solar System: A History with 22 Activities.* **Chicago Review Press, Inc., 2008.**

Learn about the solar system and the role of telescopes, satellites, probes, landers, and human missions in the history of space exploration. This book also includes 22 hands-on projects to help you learn about the planets and other celestial bodies.

Jankowski, Connie. *From Hubble to Hubble! Astronomers and Outer Space.* **Teacher Created Materials, 2008.**

Edwin Hubble changed our view of the universe. Working in an observatory, he found that there are other galaxies besides the Milky Way. He also showed that the universe is still expanding. Find out more about this amazing man here.

Jedicke, Peter. *SETI: The Search for Alien Intelligence.* **Smart Apple Media, 2003.**

Follow the continuing quest to find alien civilizations with space probes, robotics, and other new technology. This book also explores why scientists believe intelligent life beyond Earth is possible.

Stott, Carole, Robert Dinwiddie, David Hughes, and Giles Sparrow. *Space: From Earth to the Edge of the Universe.* **DK Publishing, 2010**

Experience the wonders of space from the launchpad of Earth through the planets and galaxies to the outer limits of the universe. This book features amazing photographs from NASA.

MORE TO EXPLORE

NASA Kids' Club
http://www.nasa.gov/audience/forkids/kidsclub/flash/index.html

Learn about space and NASA's missions through videos, photographs, and fun games. You can even find out what your age and weight would be on other planets.

The Rosetta Mission
http://www.esa.int/SPECIALS/Rosetta/index.html

Learn all about the European Space Agency's Rosetta mission on this website. Check out the 3D animated model, photographs, videos, and animations of the Rosetta probe.

Science News for Kids
http://www.sciencenewsforkids.org

Check out this top-notch science site with breaking news stories written just for kids. You'll find activities, links to competitions, and fascinating photos. Click on *Earth & Sky* to find the latest space stories.

Search for Extraterrestrial Intelligence
http://www.planetary.org/explore/projects/seti

This article explains what SETI is, who works on SETI, and why the program is important.

Windows to the Universe
http://www.windows2universe.org/

Explore the mysteries of Earth, our solar system, and space. This site includes a Kids' Space page where you can play fun games, get answers from scientists, and send virtual postcards to your friends with beautiful photographs of your favorite planets and scenes from space.

ABOUT THE AUTHOR

Stephanie Paris grew up in California. She received a degree in psychology from UC Santa Cruz and a teaching credential from CSU San Jose. She has been an elementary classroom teacher, an elementary school computer and technology teacher, a home-schooling mother, an educational activist, an educational author, a web designer, a blogger, and a Girl Scout leader. Ms. Paris loves to explore! She would love a chance to explore space. In the meantime, she currently lives in Germany with her husband and two children.